# Paint the Window Open

# Paint the Window Open

### Poems by

### Mary Paulson

Cover design by Shay Culligan

ISBN: 978-1-63980-031-5

Kelsay Books
502 South 1040 East, A-119
American Fork, Utah 84003
Kelsaybooks.com

*For my dad, who made this book possible*

# Acknowledgments

Thank you to the editors and readers of the following publications, where versions of these poems have appeared:

*Arkana:* "Paint the Window Open"

*Main Street Rag:* "Old Enough"

*Nerve Cowboy:* "Coda," "Ars Poetica"

*Painted Bride Quarterly:* "Dinner"

*Slow Trains:* "In the Doorbell Store," "Shine"

*Thimble Lit Magazine:* "Body Ghazal"

*Tipton Poetry Journal:* "We Would Be Gods"

# Contents

*The room is empty, And the window is open*
—Charles Simic, "My Secret Identity Is"

# In the Doorbell Store

I pressed the low buzzer
fifteen or twenty times, started
an organ chant between
like bells, a round-robin
of beautiful bells. Bright bells,
Christmas, three-note
jig bells as if to say, "we're
coming!" An announcement bell
that says, "they're here."
The promise of each
shooting through me, a stream
of electric current—
they cried out to be pressed,
not once but over and over
again. Buttons to bells
but no doors here, no one
to let in or reach out.
I rang every bell.
I'm coming! I'm here! Hello!

# Ars Poetica

There has to be room for
all of it: you, me,
my mom, dad, all our fears,
sex, death, your
ex-wife, my exes et al.

I'm measuring heaven
with a yard stick.
It spills pink orange
down the
canvas of a good god.

Certain questions
evoke the sky at this hour, the sky
and the tip of a pen
hold a thought
my hands make.

# Shine

You're all mine.
I can take you and fold you
In a velvet-lined box. I can stretch you out like a blanket
And roll myself, pulling the edge until I'm wearing you.
I can open up your chest and walk right in.
Tonight, I am very large. I grow
As though someone is pumping air into me.
I am getting bigger every day.
I shine like a freshly cleaned window.

# Old Enough

From my grandmother came my fine skin
and from her grandmother, these legs. Descendent of dark red hair,
affinity for iced vodka and certain
vulgarities: tall men with legs like tree trunks, and music,
the harpsichord in D minor.

Classical guitar on half-moon nights along the canal.
Freckles like constellations across a slight,
hooked nose. A genetically mapped fear of fire,
a pattern towards suicide and minor fainting spells.

Before cars and electric baby swings, before
whalebone corsets and clipper ships,
I danced the Follies dressed only in ostrich feathers
and a headpiece ten inches high.

I wore powdered wigs and mingled with the very rich
in ermine-trimmed wraps, satin gowns,
silk stockings that made my legs itch.

For years I lived as a farmer's wife, chasing chickens,
hanging laundry out to dry. I spun yarn
on a spindle all day and lit candles in the garret
after midnight to teach myself how to read and write.

I married an Austrian Count, had rapturous
visions of the future, was notorious for drunken,
public displays with men other than my husband.
That was the year I was burned as a witch.

In the blue pattern of my veins
you can trace the Ice Age.
In this bruise on the underside of my arm
is the thumbprint of Abraham, a suggestion of divinity
and the aspiration, if not
the perfect execution of good intentions.

This morning I'll make my way down to the water
and launch my desires like a boat out to sea.

# Blackberry

How many times have I returned to this dream—
the sun of your kiss
and your smile,
golden, riveting, so terribly hot—
your sweet, dark taste lingering
into next day—

Wanting is decadence, isn't it?
Vibratory, alive and useless—
wanting is a laser slicing vertically through my body—
from the curve at the top of my head,
it separates bone from brain, ear from ear, lung
from rib, spleen from right kidney.

# Dinner

over pepper steak I must admit
I don't like you        much
but try to pull apart
my ribs
on the way home for us

I wear a light perfume this
evening
something floral
        I can smell
with my tongue

up in your room
I'm darkly lit,
heavily guarded, held in abeyance the way you hold me—
quite on the side

my dissatisfaction with you
is gritty-sweet
a green pear offset by
gold-toothed lust

I catch myself in the long mirror
next to your bed,
        one hand holding the back of your head
bending you
                towards my mouth

# Fight

I glare blind out the window
of your red Ford.

Twist fingers in my lap, mentally
wring the heart from your heartless body—

This, our third fight of the week.

Satellite radio pours out a velvet voice.
Billie Holiday, hole in her heart big as Texas.

I glance at your profile.

Muscled jaw, straight-ahead stare,
sensuous full-fem bottom lip.

You were a junky too, years ago—

Stainless steel syringe, snowdrop
on the needle tip shivering like a dream.

I, a corrosive cokehead.

Both willful, meat-headed, we glide on our guts,
eat our own hearts—

You'd set yourself on fire just to prove me wrong
and I'm never wrong.

# Coda

The moon is in its
third quarter.
I dream it's late
and that you came
too quickly. My response
to your love sounds: winter
and freezing rain.

Lights on, I close
my eyes, see
your penis
unscrewed from your body,
left to dry on
soiled sheets.

You want to try again.
I cannot stand
touch, sound,
anything. Worms
with hurt green eyes
crawl over my skin, begging
entrance.

In the borderland,
I'm a twisting leaf,
burned orange at
the edges.

# Leaving

We sit across from each other in
agreeable conversation until dessert,

when something in the coffee
or in the bend of the sugar spoon, something
in my pathology,

causes you to cease being you
and become bigger than life—

YOU the universe, the ocean and the earth, the color violet.

Not even 8pm and already I am fastened to you
like a button, like a baby's mouth.

An o-shaped *oh* from my small mouth
when you pull off your t-shirt

as in *my oh my*
you look good
sitting on the edge of the bed.

*Oh my god* when you
graze my ribcage
with the pads of your fingers.

I like it when you call me *baby.*

The word slips like honey behind my tongue
and I pull your hand to my leg beneath the breakfast table—

Let's take the afternoon off, take a ride,
roll down the windows and play the radio loud.

Let me curl my body around your back
like a new leaf.

Years go on like this.

          There are other women who have loved you,
who still love you now,

even now, there is another woman calling,
another woman holding the line.

You say, *nonsense,* that was
someone else taking those calls, someone
not quite you

and this is a terrible dream
of falling fast through clouds,

plummeting
spine onto street.

          These days
there is no relief.

I take to sleeping during the day.

A body without skin,
all vibration,

has no place in daylight.

Without skin, without
my fingernails,

I'm a bottle of kerosene,
dirty rag, and a match
on legs. In heels.

And you say,
*you're crazy, you're crazy again.*

      You're a mean one, but I'm vile.

Following you around when *I love you*
has no meaning anymore—

when *I love you* is just obscenity.

The movers come on Wednesday
to take the dresser

and fifteen large garbage bags
containing my winter clothes.

It's great to leave you,
to walk down the hot cement sidewalk

leaving you.

# Being

I'm guilty of nothing. In the negative, my xy limitations
piss me off. I wake up dispirited, gravity bound.
Bound. In the positive, limits
prevent disruption, emotional blindness. I'm prevented
from losing my place: cog 937 million, 650,702 thousand
plus nine. I'm guilty of nothing;
just moving things about down here—
symbols, calendars, algorithms, street signs, naming conventions,
superstitions. The moon is three days dark. I'm human,
luminous, a flash like a firefly and just as important.

# We Would Be Gods

Brahma sits cross-legged on a dream of the universe.
Christ at the right hand of his Father.

Papatuanuku and Ranguini embrace
in the only darkness, only Te Kore, the Nothingness
from which they birth the world. I can't stop

this wriggling inability to settle in my skin.
My friend's gone overboard, flapping her arms

as if they were wings, quickly sinking.
My ex sees a star and jumps off the roof.

I'd like to sit like the Buddhist monks
dangling their brown toes in the dark
green current of the Tongle Sap River at dusk.

To sit on a star with my mother
and watch the moon rise above and below us.

But we get bored easily. Invariably, I leave
to watch TV. I can only see what's in my head.

Someone is chasing ghosts like a dog chasing his tail.
Someone is falling from the sky, wings on fire.

# Body Ghazal

If I cease to think, I think, I can feel my way to nothing,
no body.
Out of this aspirated knot, out of my skin, shed
my body.

Imagine instead I'm candlelit from within. This is what's left
of girlhood. Ok.
Wondrous dirty cities, moonless frozen nights, from inside
my body.

The thirty-one segments of your spinal column are rungs
on a ladder I can climb.
Because I can hear the aortic chambers of a heart like mine, I love
your body.

I'm searching for the mouth of a river that connects
one mind to another;
I try to speak, speak from my insides, not
my body.

I am as frightened in this body as I am when I take a step or two
out of it.
A hard slap from God tells me, get back in
your body.

I find myself again and again in a myriad of mundane
circumstances: washing a pot,
choosing a shirt, riding the underground trains;
a living body.

Your impassive face not loving me is the least
of my concerns, but
in terms of proximity, sleeping next to a grenade feels safer
than your body.

I decide I'll be barren. Inert, blameless, incapable
of resurrection.
I'll be the door that doesn't lead to another door,
a dead-end body.

Command the winter wait, snow stop.
Isn't that love? Each
accelerating season stands still for a moment
between our bodies.

I miss my mom. This is not the first time I've lost her but
it will be the last.
So thoughtless Mary, will you forget her face? I look at my legs
and see her body.

# Magritte's Memory

Memory seeping from mind,
only a doorbell ringing:

*recall, recall*

Walking in rain
without an umbrella

Your orange hair plastered to a forehead
all the more dear

For the face
I've forgotten

Perhaps here we walked,
here we ate

Sharp onion soup, thick
white bread

Here we argued forgiveness
all the way down 19th Street

Before turning left, disappearing
into the summer fog

On a night like tonight
streetlights shrouded in smoke

I might meet myself
walking off the earth with you—

# Paint the Window Open

For cheekbone, upper bow of lip—
use thick, muscular oil paints

and for her thoughts,
descending shades pink—

pale dogwood, coral, tea rose, deep Persian.
Apply the paint straight from the tube

and use a stiff bristle brush.
Paint her lying uncovered in a circle

of late afternoon sun, supine
on an unmade bed.

Paint her dark eyes
watching the fan spin its slow circles

on the vaulted ceiling of a
large, windowed room.

Add a wood frame bed, side table,
stool, and dresser—all surfaces cluttered—

jewelry and empty jewelry boxes, coins
loose papers, notebooks, pens.

Small islands of discarded clothing dotting the floor.
Paint her rolling on to her side—scar

on the back of her shoulder shaped
like a slim silver fish. Make her

long hair heavy, Turkish coffee dark,
fingernails short and nude.

Paint her to be everything you wish
you could have been—

tragic and beautiful, adored
and admired, radiating depth, *alive.*

Use extreme, saturated color for your rage,
at middle-age, brown spots, loose

skin, promises mangled and flattened in dust,
for the bit lip, blood taste of a cry withheld,

for the desperation to be still lovelier, more
poignant, better than you turned out to be.

Paint the window open.
Use a fine, Kolinsky sable brush.

# About the Author

Mary Paulson's poems have appeared in *Nerve Cowboy, Slow Trains, Mainstreet Rag, Painted Bride Quarterly, Thimble Lit Magazine, Arkana,* and *Tipton Poetry Journal.* She currently resides in Naples, FL.

Made in the USA
Columbia, SC
08 October 2021